NEW YORK REVIEW COMICS

PRETENDING IS LYING

DOMINIQUE GOBLET was born in 1967 in Brussels, Belgium, and studied illustration at St. Luke's Institute. Known for her wide range of artistic mediums and eclectic style of visual storytelling, she was an early contributor to the comics publisher Fréon's anthology *Frigorevue*. Involved from the start in the creation of the experimental comics publisher Frémok, she published several books with them: *Portraits crachés* (1997), *Souvenir d'une journée parfaite* (2002), and *Les hommes-loups* (2010). At the same time she worked with the Parisian publishing house L'Association and published two books with them: *Pretending Is Lying* (2007) and *Chronographie* (2010), a book of double portraits of her and her daughter made once a week for ten years; both received a number of nominations and prizes, including the EESI award at the Angoulème festival and the Prix Töpffer. Most recently she has published *Plus si entente* (Actes Sud BD/Frémok), a collaboration with the Berlin artist Kai Pfeiffer. Artist, comics author, and professor of comics and illustration, she is also certified as an electrician, plumber, and welder.

SOPHIE YANOW is a cartoonist and translator. She is the author of *War of Streets and Houses* and was a fellow at the Center for Cartoon Studies in White River Junction, Vermont.

PRETENDING IS LYING

Dominique Goblet

Translated by

SOPHIE YANOW

in collaboration with the author

NEW YORK REVIEW COMICS · *New York*

THIS IS A NEW YORK REVIEW COMIC
PUBLISHED BY THE NEW YORK REVIEW OF BOOKS
435 Hudson Street, New York, NY 10014
www.nyrb.com

The text of chapters 2 and 4 was co-written with Guy Marc Hinant.
The author would like to acknowledge the support of the Communauté Français Wallonie-Bruxelles, and the support of the Centre National du Livre, Paris, France.

English lettering by Dominique Goblet.

Cet ouvrage a bénéficié du soutien des Programmes d'aide à la publication de l'Institut Français.

This work, published as part of a program of aid for publication, received support from the Institut Français.

A catalog record for this book is available from the Library of Congress

ISBN 978-1-68137-047-7
Available as an electronic book; ISBN 978-1-68137-048-4

Printed in the United States of America
2 4 6 8 0 9 7 5 3 1

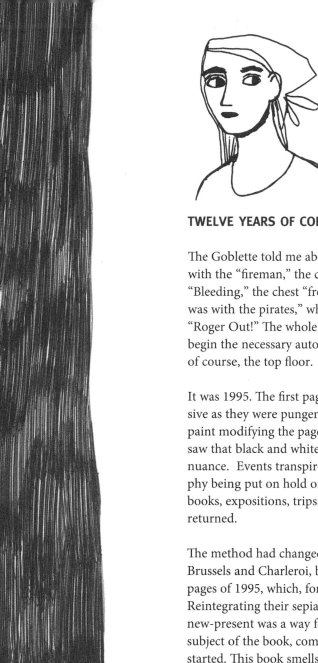

TWELVE YEARS OF CORRECTIONS

The Goblette told me about the famous day: the drunk reunion with the "fireman," the colored pencils that Nikita already had, "Bleeding," the chest "from when I brought back from when I was with the pirates," which collapsed, the Turbo injection . . . "Roger Out!" The whole thing, you know? The perfect scene to begin the necessary autobiography, and to attempt to arrive at, of course, the top floor.

It was 1995. The first pages of the first chapter were as impressive as they were pungent. Each time I saw them, there was oil paint modifying the pages. This troubled me a little, because I saw that black and white wouldn't suffice for rendering such nuance. Events transpired which resulted in the autobiography being put on hold on multiple occasions. There were other books, expositions, trips; the autobiography returned, left again, returned.

The method had changed: grey pencils now steadily rendered Brussels and Charleroi, but it was the same story from the pages of 1995, which, for their part, had continued to yellow. Reintegrating their sepia tone and their now-old style with the new-present was a way for Dom to defy time, the true first subject of the book, completed twelve years after it was started. This book smells of oil, grease pencil, humid wood, the disorder of the street market; it exhales twelve years of well-tempered promises, carefully untied and resolutely wrapped up. *Pretending Is Lying* breathes like no other book.

JEAN-CHRISTOPHE MENU
Editor of original L'Association edition

INTRODUCTION

careful NiKsKe
you're going to

Did you get hurt?
Holes! Holes! Oh noooo holes!!!
Holes here! HERE! holes! holes! holes, oohohhh!
Ohhohhhh
OKay, come here, let's take these off!

It's not the end of the world, look, i'm going to fix them!
She...
She can do magic...

CHAPTER 1

MY FATHER DOESN'T DRINK ANYMORE. NOT ONE MORE DROP, SUPPOSEDLY. I HAVEN'T SEEN HIM IN FOUR YEARS. MY DAUGHTER WILL BE FOUR IN JULY... NEXT MONTH, THAT IS
What's he like?
Um... well, he has a big mustache
Hello!
Well!
Well!
Well!
Well! look who's here!
This is Nikita, she's asked a ton of questions about you

UCCLE 81
Mommy... I'm going to tell you a secret
I'm going to call him Grandpa Mustache
Did you know he invited us over for dinner tomorrow?
But actually Mommy, why did you stop seeing your daddy?

HEYYY!
I must be dreaming, they're drunk, they're dead drunk
We bought colored pencils but we Forgot to bring Paper!
Hello Blandine !!
Oh, isn't that nice! Aren't you happy, Nikita?
I'm not really i already have some...
Hello Nikske*, So, what do you think of my new private parking spot?
Umm... Nice! very nice, very fancy!
IN BRUSSELS DIALECT, THIS DIMINUTIVE OF DOMINIQUE MEANS: "LITTLE NOTHING"
My neighbor loves me Y'know!! He loves me!! I go out... he loves me he actually offered, to let me park there!
You aren't afraid of dogs, right? cuz Kimi loves children. Right, look, i go for a walk, right, She sees a kid, She crosses the street. What an unbelievable dog!!!
YAP YAP YAP YAP
And my next-door neighbor... he loves me!
Watch this, i trade my "MOSQUITO-TV" magazine for my next-door neighbor's "ENTERTAINMENT WEEKLY"!

Here's the beast!
I mean, a beautiful animal right, 25 lbs!
That is a good animal. Not like the doberman
But one day, he bit my ear, well, that may have been my own fault a little!
That animal wasn't made to play, I'd riled him up a bit.
I was wrestling with him.

YES! AND AFTER, IT BIT ME ON THE NECK AND RIGHT HERE, JUST LIKE THAT, FOR NO GOOD REASON !!!
Hey who's telling this story ME OR YOU?
Next day, i put him down. Even though that dog loved me. Obeyed my every word. But one day he just went crazy.
Yeah well... this one's headed for trouble too...
I called Veeweyde* They wanted to take the body. NO WAY. COME ON! Don't mess with me huh!
* ANIMAL SHELTER
TAKE THE BODY HUH? way to go! VEEWEYDE!
HOW's about BEFORE we take him, you let us know he was a night guard dog in a parking lot and he was dangerous that they couldn't do huh!!!
Oof, Grandpa Mustache you sure speak baaad !!

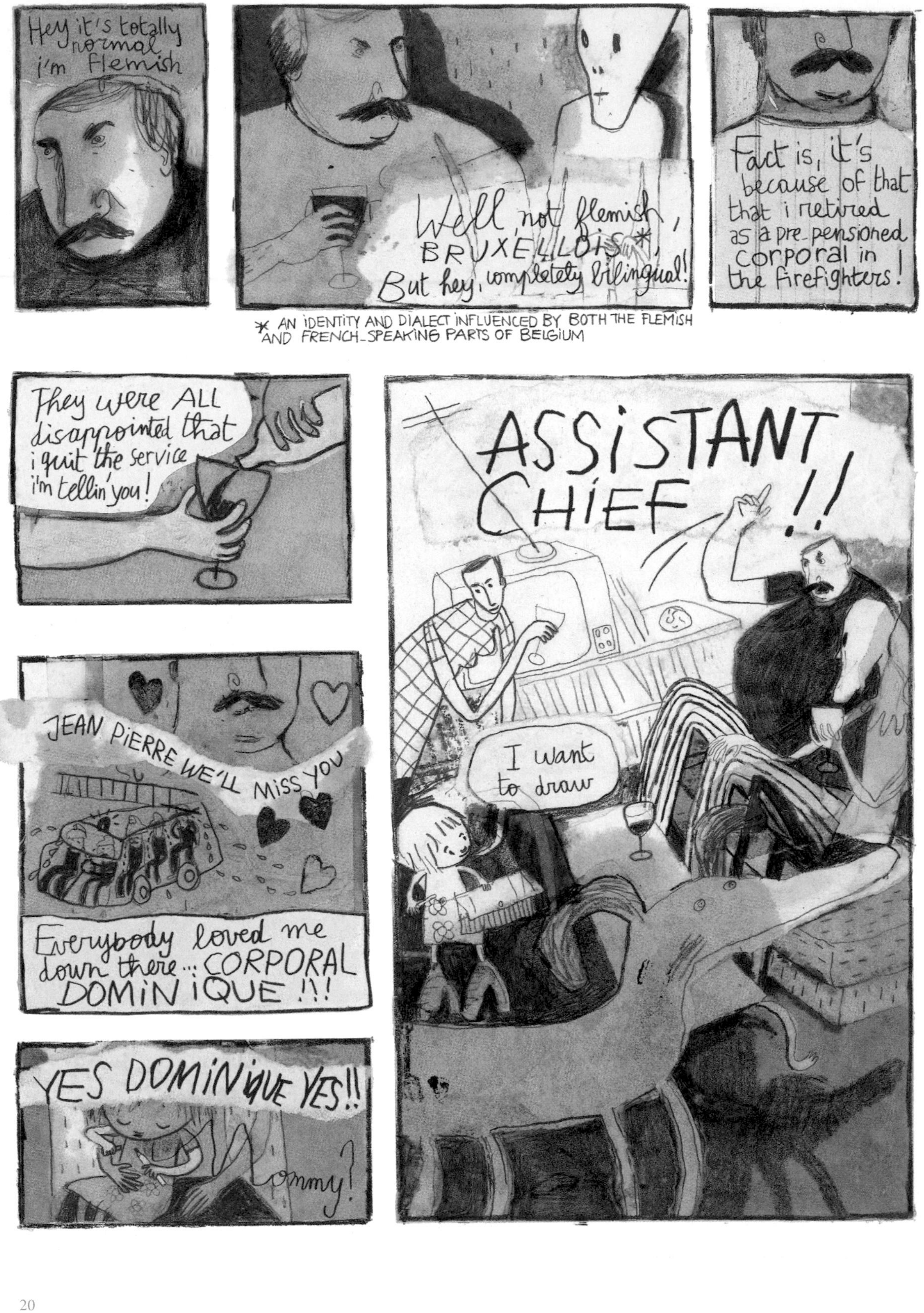
Hey it's totally normal i'm Flemish
Well, not flemish, BRUXELLOIS*, But hey, completely bilingual!
Fact is, it's because of that that i retired as a pre-pensioned corporal in the firefighters!
* AN IDENTITY AND DIALECT INFLUENCED BY BOTH THE FLEMISH AND FRENCH-SPEAKING PARTS OF BELGIUM
They were ALL disappointed that i quit the service i'm tellin' you!
JEAN PIERRE WE'LL MISS YOU
Everybody loved me down there... CORPORAL DOMINIQUE!!!
ASSISTANT CHIEF!!
I want to draw
YES DOMINIQUE YES!!
Mommy?

Here Nik, gotcha something to draw on!
Haaa... That's a mistake too!
That what ?
"Gotcha" ... It's dialect!
C'mon Dad no it's not!
No! No! "Gotcha" isn't proper We say: Got It & You
Well, to me it just seems like a contraction
OK Dominique, enough, i get it, done, fine, i don't want to argue any more with you, ROGER OUT! anyhow it's always been like this, you're just like your mother, just the same!

Here, see her hair ... That's my friend !!!
Ah, does your friend have long hair?
Well no why?
WELL WHAT IS IT THEN?
You just said that it's your friend and that she has long hair!!
Ha, nope, it's just a character!
PRETENDING IS LYING IT'S LYING!
PRETENDING IS LYING!
Hey, NiKita, Blandine is right, you said that it was
Yeah well sure, but that was just for pretend!
Well Then You are a LIAR!
am not!

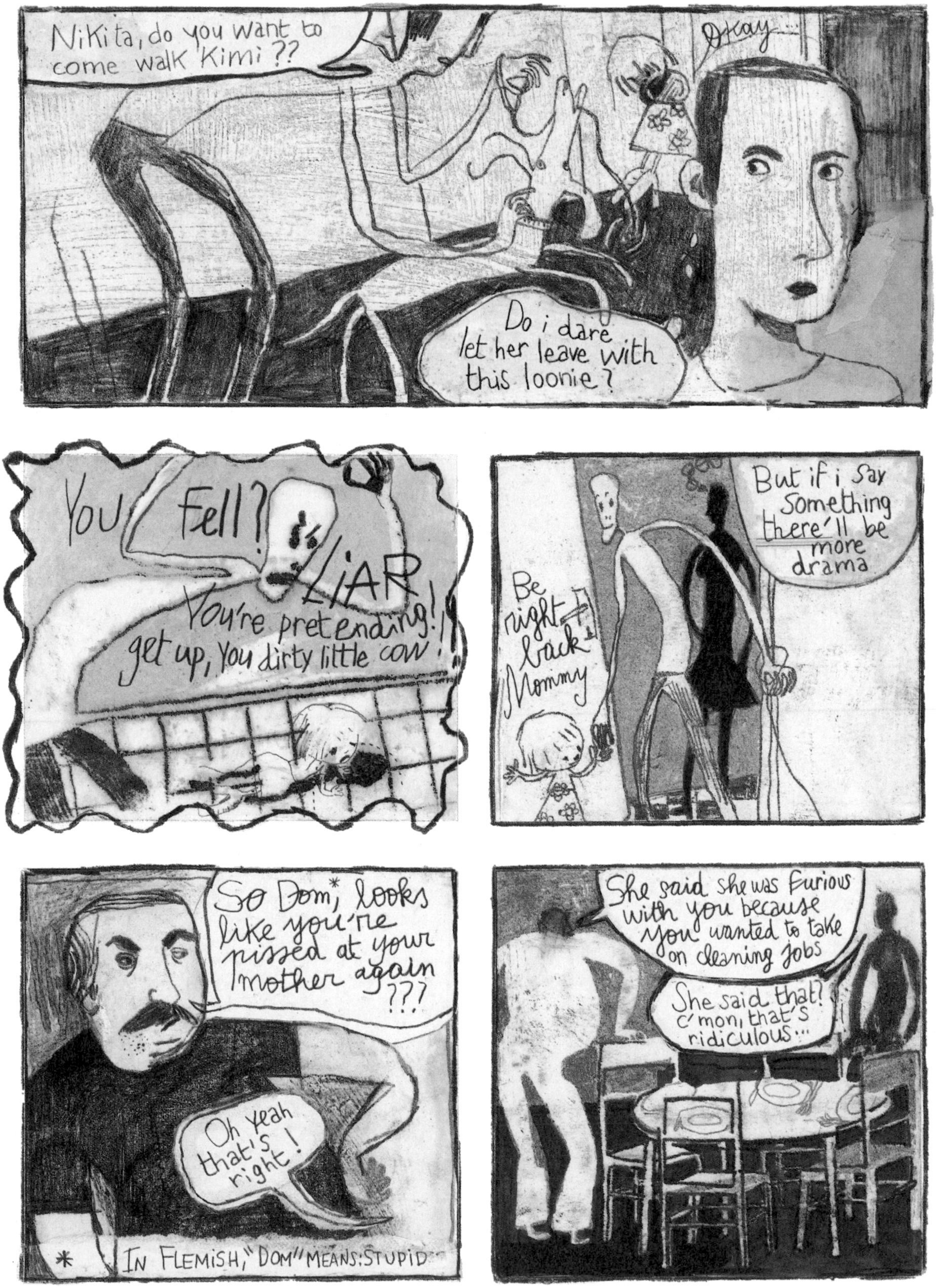
Nikita, do you want to come walk Kimi??
Okay...
Do i dare let her leave with this loonie?
You Fell?
LiAR!
You're pretending!! get up, You dirty little cow!
But if i say something there'll be more drama
Be right back Mommy
So Dom*, looks like you're pissed at your mother again???
Oh yeah that's right!
* IN FLEMISH, "DOM" MEANS: STUPID
She said she was furious with you because you wanted to take on cleaning jobs
She said that? c'mon, that's ridiculous...

Yeah... Your mother's one of a kind Huh...
Hey, you seen this yet??
Uh no...
CRACK!
This is the chest from when i brought back from when i was with the pirates!
Come on, you're not gonna tell me... She's one of a Kind right!

You Know she called me the very same day it was over with her stud?
That's What i'm Good for Huh!!
Anyway she always did whatever she wanted!
AND YOU?
AND, YOU? WELL! Dominique...
YOU, YOU, YOU MADE A GOOD TEAM WITH HER

Yeah, yeah, you two really abandoned me!
AND I DID EVERYTHING FOR YOU TWO
I always took care of my responsibilities
I GAVE YOU EVERYTHING I DID EVERYTHING FOR YOU!
I WORKED LIKE A SLAVE!! DAY AND NIGHT... did everything!! ALL... ALL for the two of you!
everything!

Well, true, or false?
But me Dominique What did i get from you???
And when she left, who, Who had to take care of you
??
It's me... true or false?
Didn't you have little sandwiches every day for school?

I did everything for you!
Yes well,
That said...
That said, that said...
Thaaaat said Thaaaat said
Thaaaaaat said... you're not gonna come here and get stuck up with me!!
Oh c'mon Papa, i didn't say anything fancy!
You with your U-Ni-VER-Si-TY langage!
Thaaaaaa said...
Yeah well what i wanted to say is that it's really the most basic duty for parents to feed their children...
ME, i HAVE NO DUTiES, NO OBLiGATiONS !!!
Well, there are laws, aren't there?
NO DUTiES!! Nobody lays down the law with me!!!

At the very least do you know how much i gave her in alimony?
That doesn't concern me
Oh yeah that's easy, "That doesn't concern me!"
But when she left me and had her escapades in the Ardennes, WHERE did she stay?
And don't go and say you don't know huh?!?
"That doesn't concern me!"
Yeah
Yeah, that doesn't concern me! LOOK at how you are!
That doesn't concern me!
That doesn't concern me ... You've ALWAYS been a team with her!!!
That doesn't concern me...
She really raised you against me
And you just abandoned me!
That's how it is, no question!
Anyway it's pretty simple you didn't even come see me when i was in the hospital last year
But you knew i was sick huh?!
Listen, it's been four years since you bothered to see me, so why should i come running because you decide to wreck your health?

Wreck my health? ...What are you even talking about??
I'm talking about drinking. You had liver damage and internal hemorrhaging because you drank too much!!!
NO DOMINIQUE, NO THAT'S NOT IT AT ALL!!!
Oh no? i ran into you in the street a year ago You couldn't keep yourself up. Blandine had to hold you up to walk.
We were only a meter from each other and you didn't even recognize me!
FALSE DOMINIQUE, ABSOLUTELY FALSE! I no longer drank a single drop!
CUT IT OUT, You've always drunk!
Hey, with what i went through, it's perfectly normal to drink!

Look at those arguments with your mom. I don't go through that anymore, you know...
Make no mistake huh, with Blandine too sometimes we exchange words
And then we each sulk in our own corner
But an hour later it's over!
No Dominique no... that was no kind of life!
But anyhow, me, i've always taken care of my responsibilities
And i was ALWAYS a good father!
True OR FALSE?
In truth... a remarkable father!
You know it's thanks to me you always had something to eat on your plate!
True... or not true?
Well yeah, that's true!

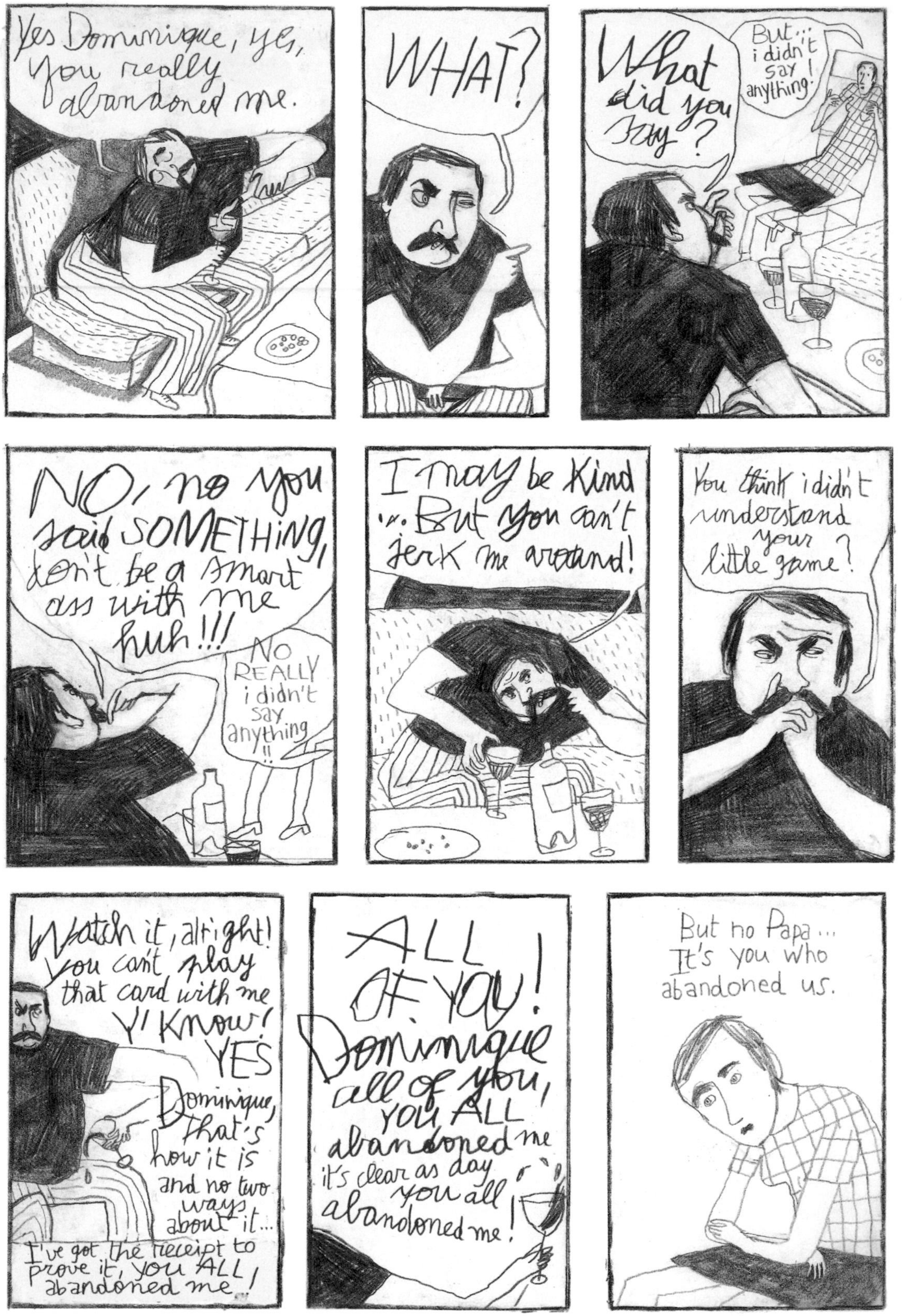
Yes Dominique, yes, you really abandoned me.
WHAT?
What did you say?
But... i didn't say anything!
NO, no you said SOMETHING, don't be a smart ass with me huh!!!
NO REALLY i didn't say anything !!
I may be Kind ... But you can't Jerk me around!
You think i didn't understand your little game?
Watch it, alright! You can't play that card with me Y'Know! YES Dominique, That's how it is and no two ways about it...
I've got the receipt to prove it, you ALL abandoned me!
ALL OF YOU! Dominique all of you, YOU ALL abandoned me it's clear as day you all abandoned me!
But no Papa... It's you who abandoned us.

CHAPTER 2

Anyway, my father is above all a rational person

He was still young at the time and was going with his mother to the coast. She had rented a house in Ostende.
During the night, they heard the doors and windows slamming about upstairs
He thought that maybe it was a gust of wind, he closed them one by one...
But an hour later, they were open again
This time, my father went up, closed them again and checked to see if one of them was busted
He was just back downstairs when they reopened for no apparent reason, all of them, one after another...

The dog got anxious and began to bark
Then there was a noise, just once, a muted noise, and the dog began to howl like mad
My father went back up, and closed all the windows again, for the third time. Believe me, he was really shaken up!!
He took the dog, it was a fox terrier and there, ... in front of a door, the dog stopped short!!
It sniffed under the door and its hair stood on end. I can tell you, that night, my father had a hard time getting to sleep
So he got up and felt his way towards the window to look at the dunes...
And it's at that very moment that he heard a sort of sucking sound ... right by his ear.

And for a fraction of a second, he felt an icy liquid going through his body
He had to turn the lights back on, he was panicked, his teeth were chattering ... In the silence of the night, he heard a muffled grunt. It was the dog on the ground floor.
Gulp... Do you want another drink ?
Ah no. I'd rather we leave, i'm a little hungry... if you want, we could go to your place and i'll fix you a nice meal !

Do you want some coffee? i just made a thermos

All this racket doesn't bother Dad?
Oh you know, he doesn't complain

How is he ??

He's fine...

Hey i met a girl

Oh really ? What's she like ??
I like her ... a lot ... i don't know ... She's special !
That's all we want, to finally see our son happy with somebody !

Is she pretty?
Yes, really pretty! i mean, i think so

I hope we'll see her soon!

Well, okay i'm going to go

ZEEMAN
OUTLET
PARKING

What are you thinking of making ??
Sautee some vegetables, some rice, maybe a chicken curry...
Something good and simple!
That's all? You think we'll be done by tomorrow?
Wait, are you actually single?
Single? Yes, yes well i was with a girl for two years
... But now, i'm single yes...
You don't think it's ... Um, a bit too much?

EIEREN
CAISS
Too much? No, i love cooking ... and eating! don't you??
Yes but it has to be quick, otherwise what a waste of time!
Well then, what do you usually eat? give me an example of a dish you make sometimes...
When my son is home, i might make pasta with tuna, for example
It seems like a simple recipe but actually it isn't quite so easy...
First of all, you have to fill a saucepan with water
When it's boiling, bam! you throw in the pasta in one go
And at that moment, you open a can of tuna. There are many brands. But in general i get "Starkist"
CHARC
BIERES

There is one with vegetables, it's not bad!
There are many possible versions: with oil, without oil, it's your choice...
And then, you see, you have to open a second can, tomato sauce this time
To know if the pasta is ready, you have to pay attention... At least, i don't trust the time written on the box...
...I take out a few noodles with a fork and taste them. If they're ready, i run them under cold water
When they're just about "al dente", you taste them, and you put them back in the pan and there you mix everything up, and you can add salt, spices, etc if you have them... and you plop it all onto soup plates.
EXQUISITE... AND FAST !!!

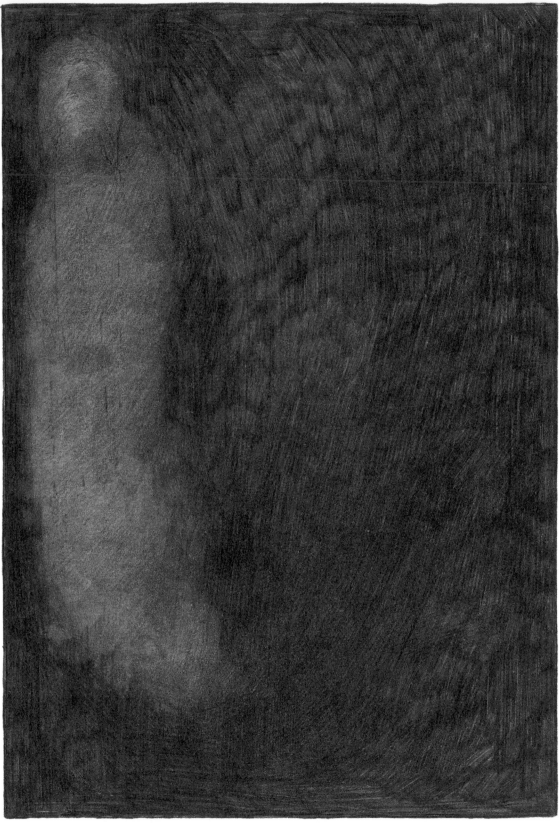

AVENUE
du
Diamant

It doesn't tire you out to work like this? 2PM ... It's a bad time for work, do you know how many workers hurt themselves at this very hour??

Go on, get out, Mustache!
Someone called a few times ... But when i answer, they hang up! It's really annoying and unpleasant ...
I've had that type of thing happen, mistakes sometimes ...
But i seem to hear breathing. There's someone on the other end ...
Listen, if that happens again, don't pick up, let the answering machine get it, and don't worry yourself over it !!

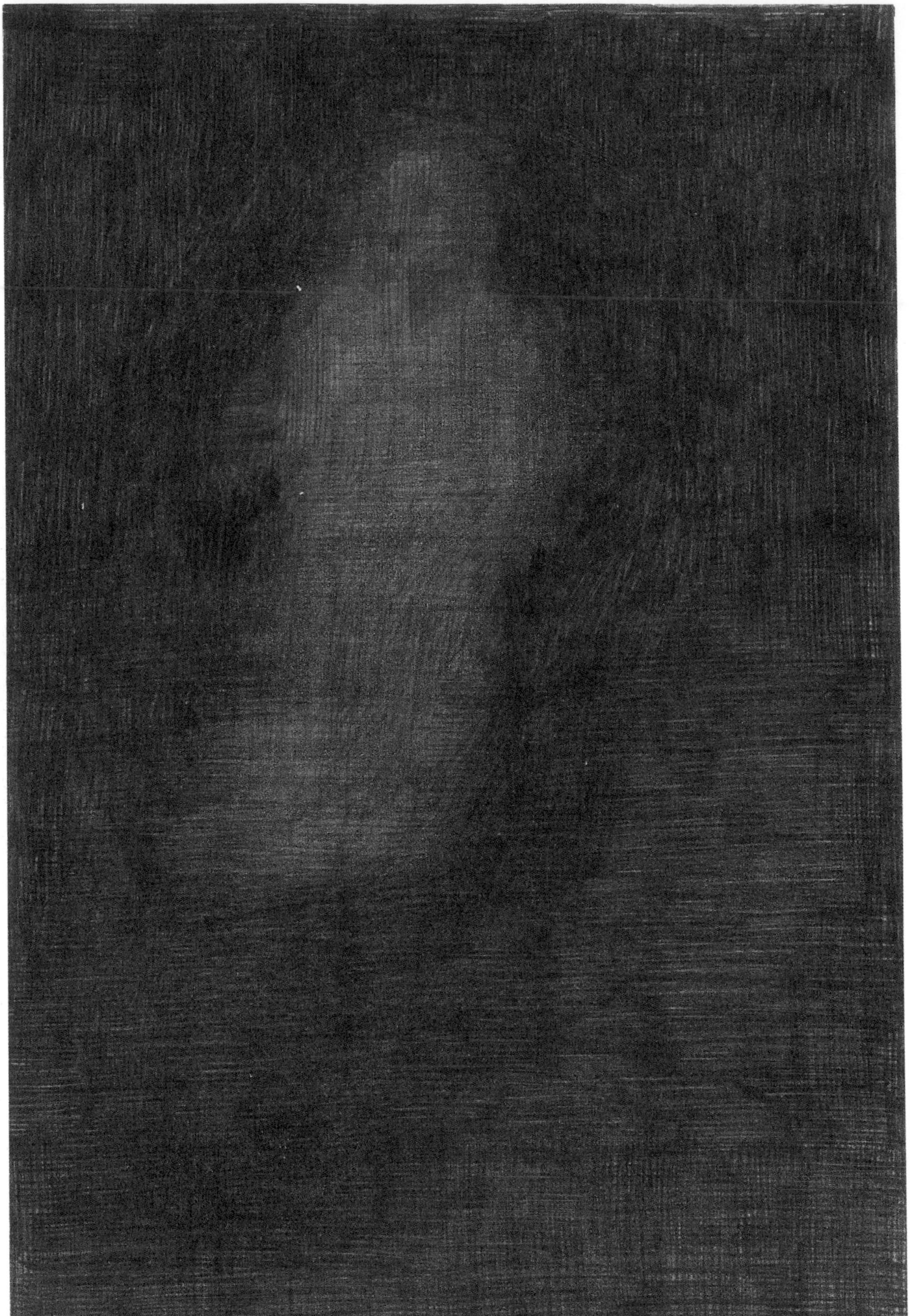

Aghh!
I've had enough!!!
Are you okay? is it the TV station?
Honestly, i'm going to give up, i wasn't made for this...
Calm down, we're going to spend a lovely evening together look...
Listen, there are other things in life besides the day-to-day, all of this is great but really, it's going nowhere... It seems like i don't have time to do anything. I'm stuck... i do a million things and nothing comes out...
Ah well, bon appetit... nonetheless!
RRING!
ah... coming...

RRING
Hello?!?
... Can you hang on for a second?
CLAC
OKay
Sorry, but well, She... Yeah you know how it is...
How long did i wait? and what did you do??
nothing.
I know it's complicated...
But if only you had made some kind of decision, i wouldn't have ... But here we are...

You throw that at me, and you dare to tell me we can't see each other? It's madness!!
Well me neither, you know, i can't take it anymore !! You should understand!!
Ah... is the tea ready?
But... That's all you have to say?
It was her... the girl i told you about. I guess you figured that. She ... but don't worry, i'm going to work out the problem ... actually, there isn't a problem ... it's nothing but memories. But... How can i put it... i don't like that she treats me this way, like that, it's too much! even if it's over, ... There's only so much i can take !!
But when it's really over ... Does one still cry?

How long is NiK staying with us?
Well, until sunday, as usual, Harvey will come by to pick her up from my place
And Xavier, when is he coming back?
I dunno, right now he prefers to stay with his mother
Well in that case, i can let her sleep in Xa's bed
mm... Okay!
Mommy, i don't like being here, that THING scares me

You Know, You shouldn't be afraid of it. This is called "the laugh". When we see it, we have to laugh at him, you can point at him... You have to laugh at the things that scare you, you'll see, it works with everything!

pff...

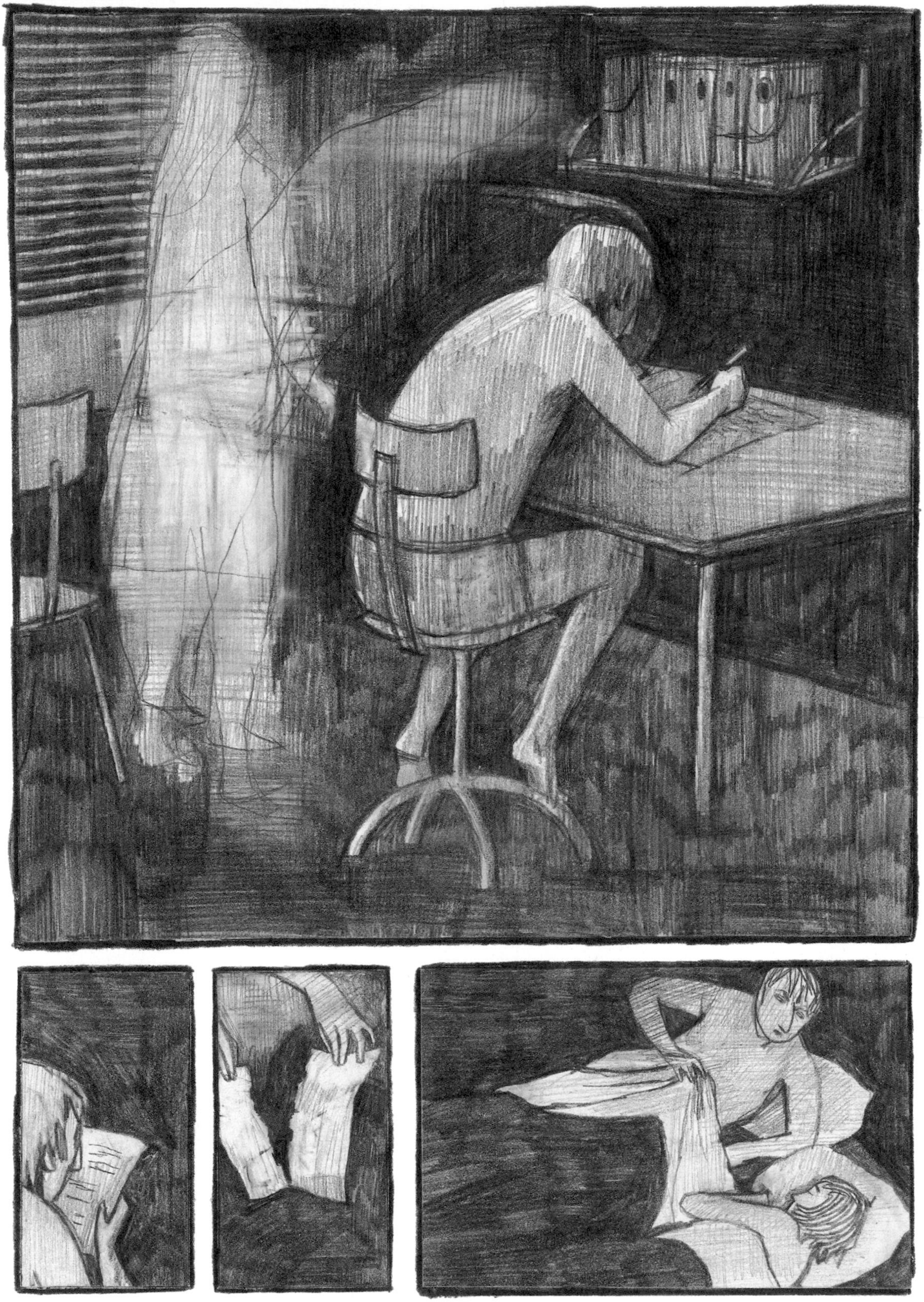

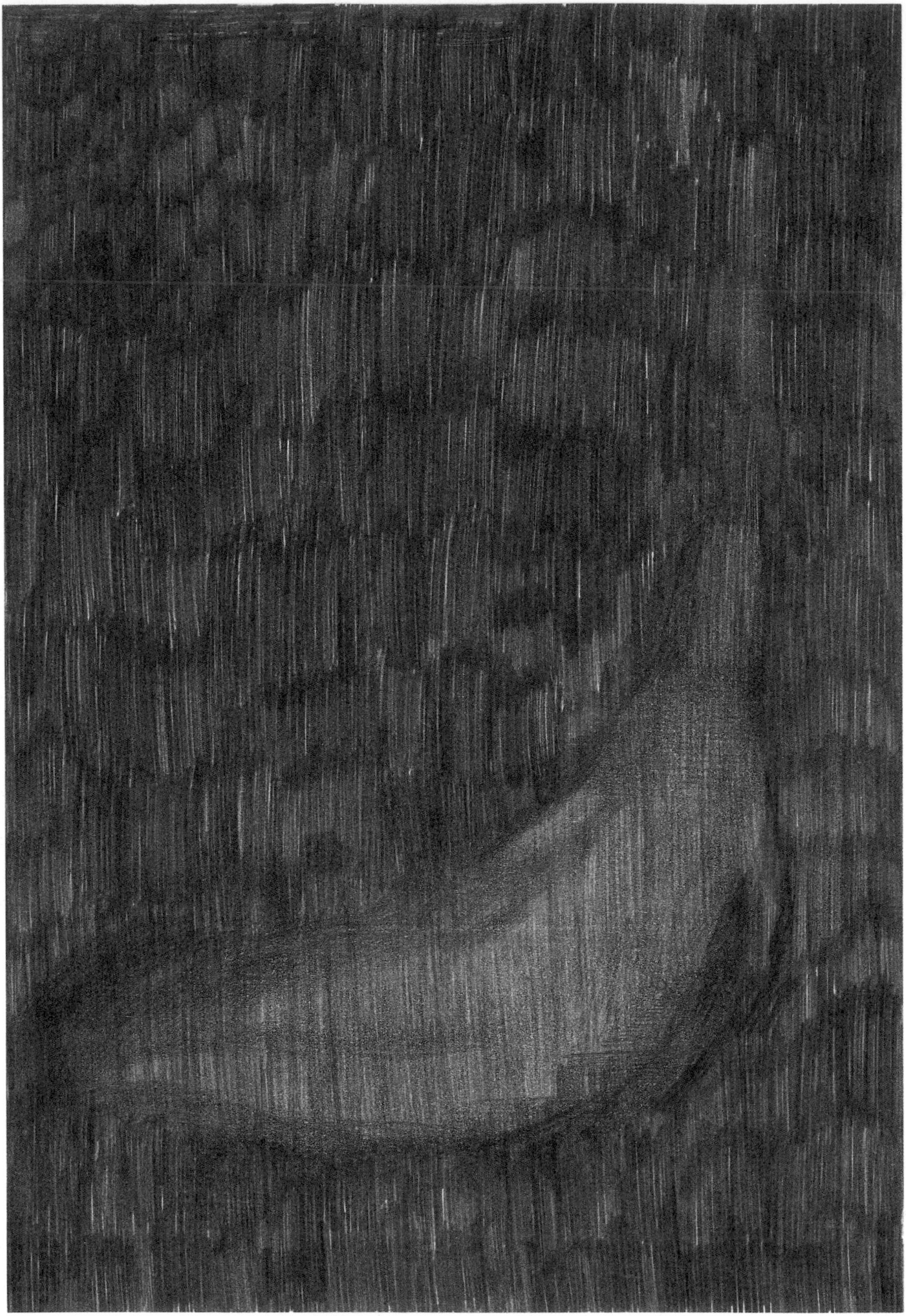

Don't worry, i'm just covering a short shift, i won't be there for hours... have a nice night...
Oh man... my head is Killing me...
BAZAARS OF INDIA
He's not there? But i thought that ... ah well, goodbye!!

no...
This hurts me ... You know i love you, but nothing's possible now...
I feel empty ... like a part of me has died
You can't talk like that
I feel like my life is over, and i can't do anything about it ...
How did we get here? Why did you leave me like this, when things were starting to work out?
You must know that you're the one i love and nobody else!
But then why do you live with him and not me?
But you have someone right now too. We can't always choose...

But look at him and look at me!!
There's nobody but you, you know that... we're the only ones who can understand that
HELLO, ANYbody home ??
How are you?
Where were you?
Well, at work, why?
I called, you weren't there!?!
At the TV station? of course! I wasn't there... I didn't say i was doing the broadcast. i had to prepare it, do the preparations you know
It's not worth overdramatizing, what's gotten into you?... What's the problem? Quit it for a second alright!...
I had an ocular migraine, i was totally blind for half an hour. I wanted you to come back.
You know what? we'll buy a cell phone that way there'll be no more misunderstandings !!

RIGHT, well, time to get to it!!

What are you doing??
I'm writing a new piece...
on?
A hypothetical encounter between Brian Wilson and Thomas Pynchon
→ But before the call promised by the journalist to set up a meeting (one call too many) Pynchon contemplates an impromptu little visit outside Manhattan Beach, L.A. immediately.
... → for this track (these fragments we'll organize later), Brian wears a metal California State Firefighter's helmet, certain harmonies make him think of fire — This magic (and the acid that he is absorbing) creates the fire ...

...But soon he feels responsible for the fires that spread throughout the city, stops everything and erases the recordings...

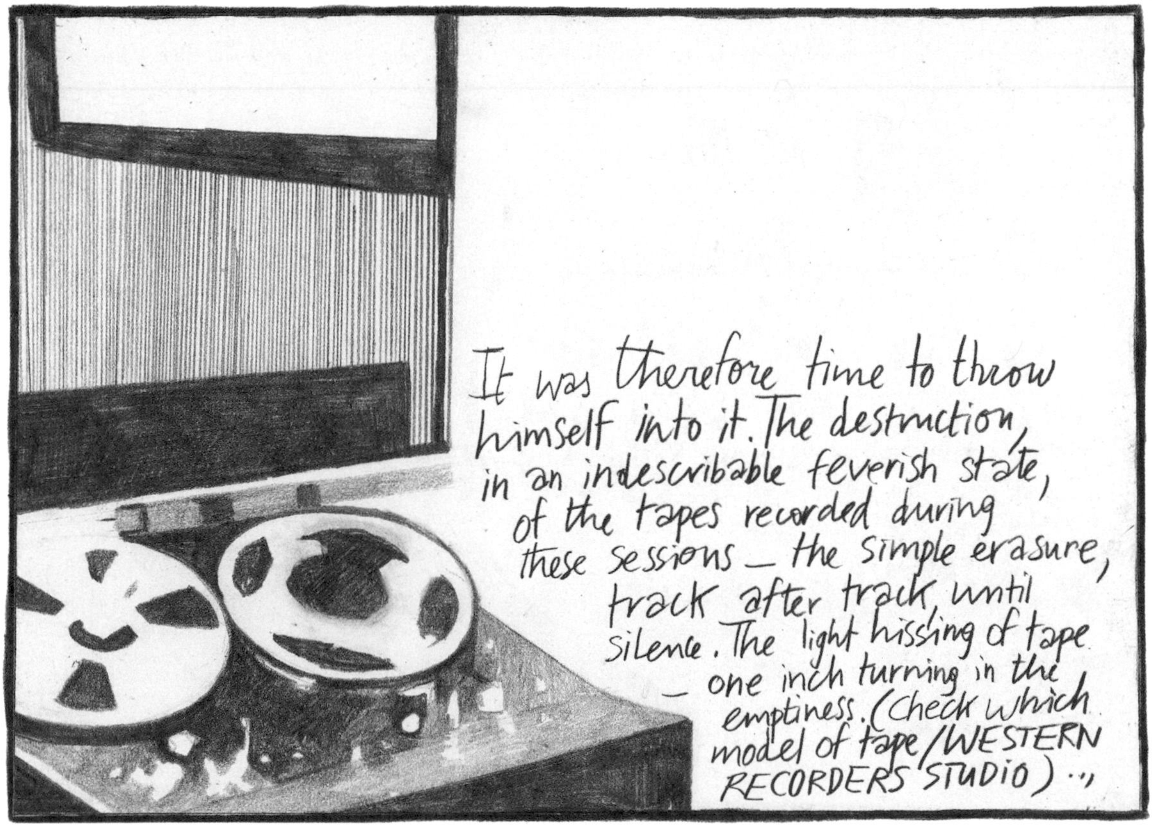
It was therefore time to throw himself into it. The destruction, in an indescribable feverish state, of the tapes recorded during these sessions – the simple erasure, track after track, until silence. The light hissing of tape – one inch turning in the emptiness. (Check which model of tape/WESTERN RECORDERS STUDIO)...

My work is coming along, but i definitely can't finish tonight. Can i take you to a movie? Would you like that?
What's with you? Do you know her or what?
What are you talking about? What have i done this time?
I'm starting to get sick of your stories, alright?
Woah, back off a little! i really don't see what i did that...
AREMBERG-GALERIES
2
COU
R
Take me home please!
Why??
Guess!
Well good timing, i need to be alone. All this jealousy makes me dizzy. If only it were justified!!
Can you please just take me home?

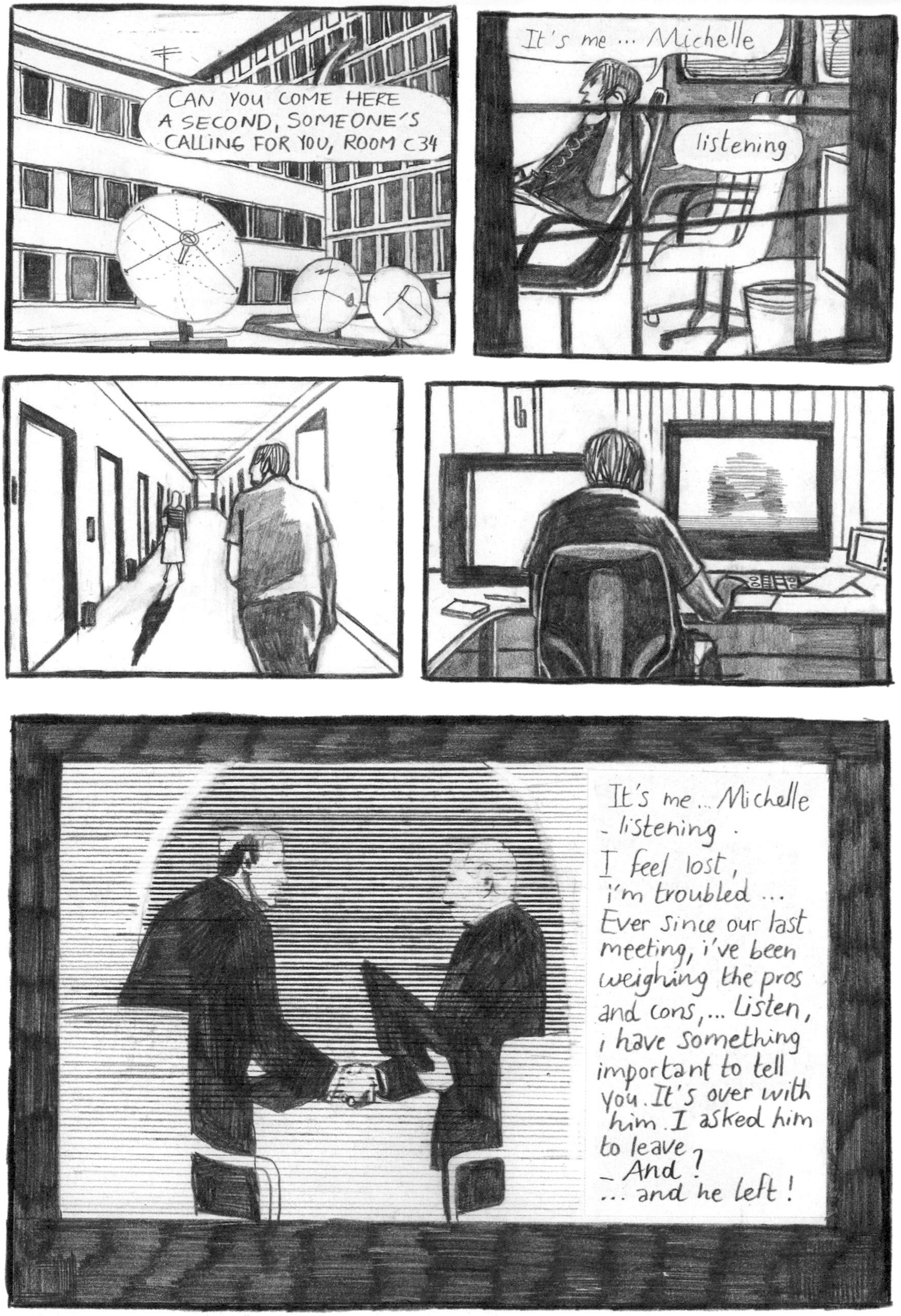
CAN YOU COME HERE A SECOND, SOMEONE'S CALLING FOR YOU, ROOM C34
It's me ... Michelle
listening
It's me ... Michelle
_ listening .
I feel lost,
i'm troubled ...
Ever since our last meeting, i've been weighing the pros and cons, ... Listen, i have something important to tell you. It's over with him. I asked him to leave.
_ And ?
... and he left !

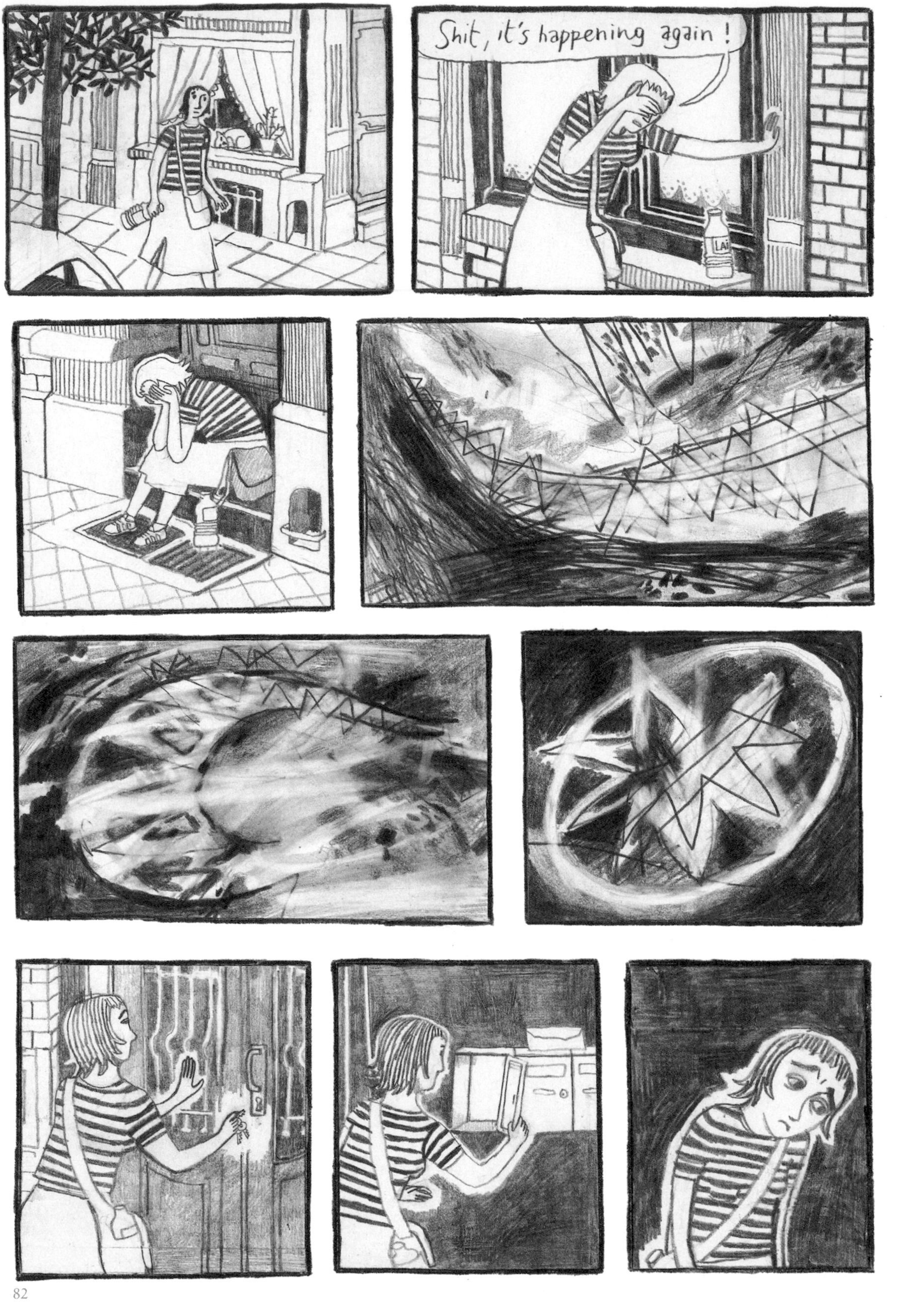
Shit, it's happening again!
LAIT

Three migraines in two weeks ... i'm going to go crazy
What's he doing?
Should i go ... or not? no i really shouldn't go ...
6:35
How's it going?
Not great ... You?
It's been five days since we saw each other, i couln't take it anymore, i had to come, i had to see you

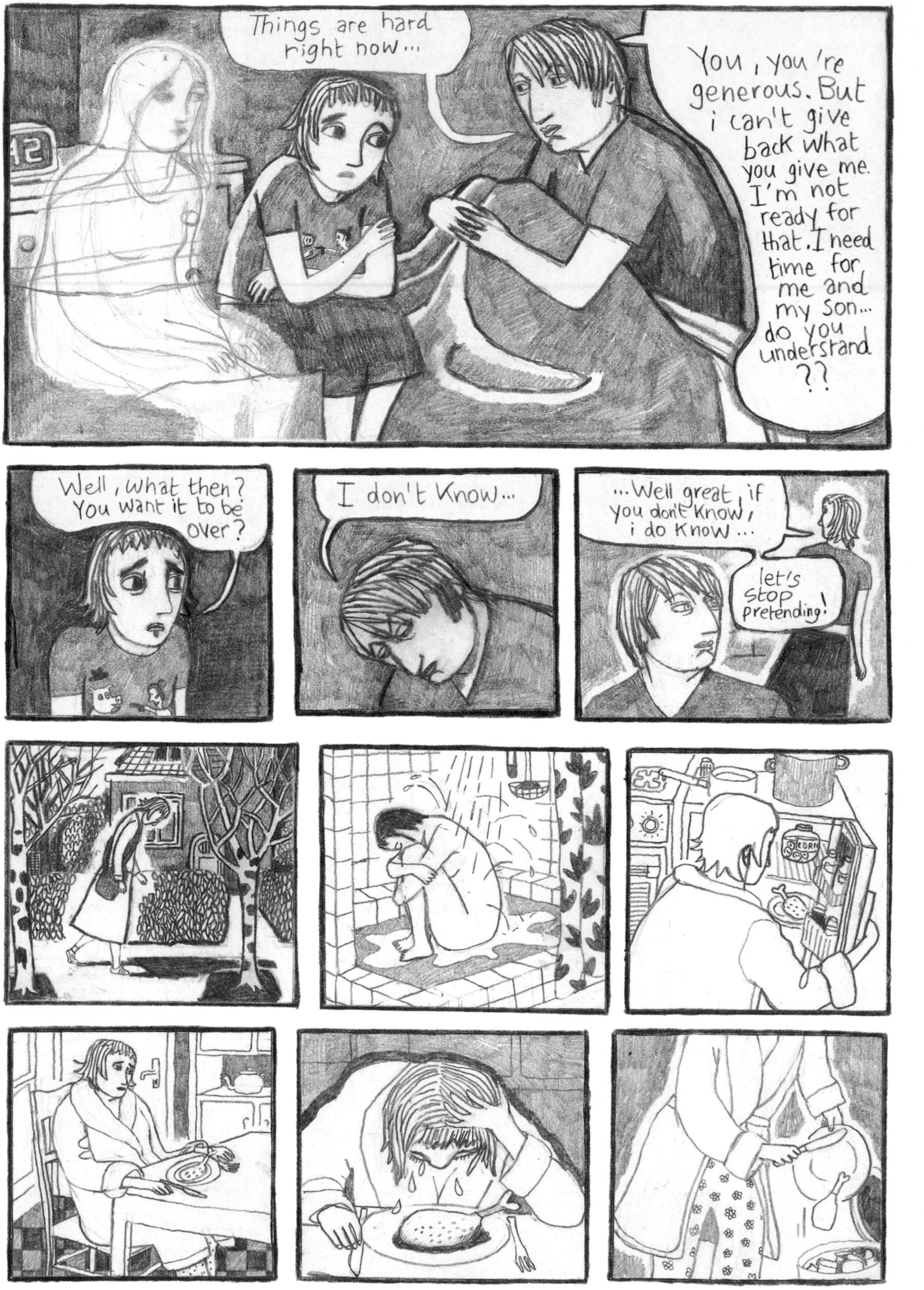
Things are hard right now...
You, you're generous. But i can't give back what you give me. I'm not ready for that. I need time for me and my son... do you understand??
Well, what then? You want it to be over?
I don't Know...
...Well great, if you don't Know, i do Know...
let's stop pretending!
CORN

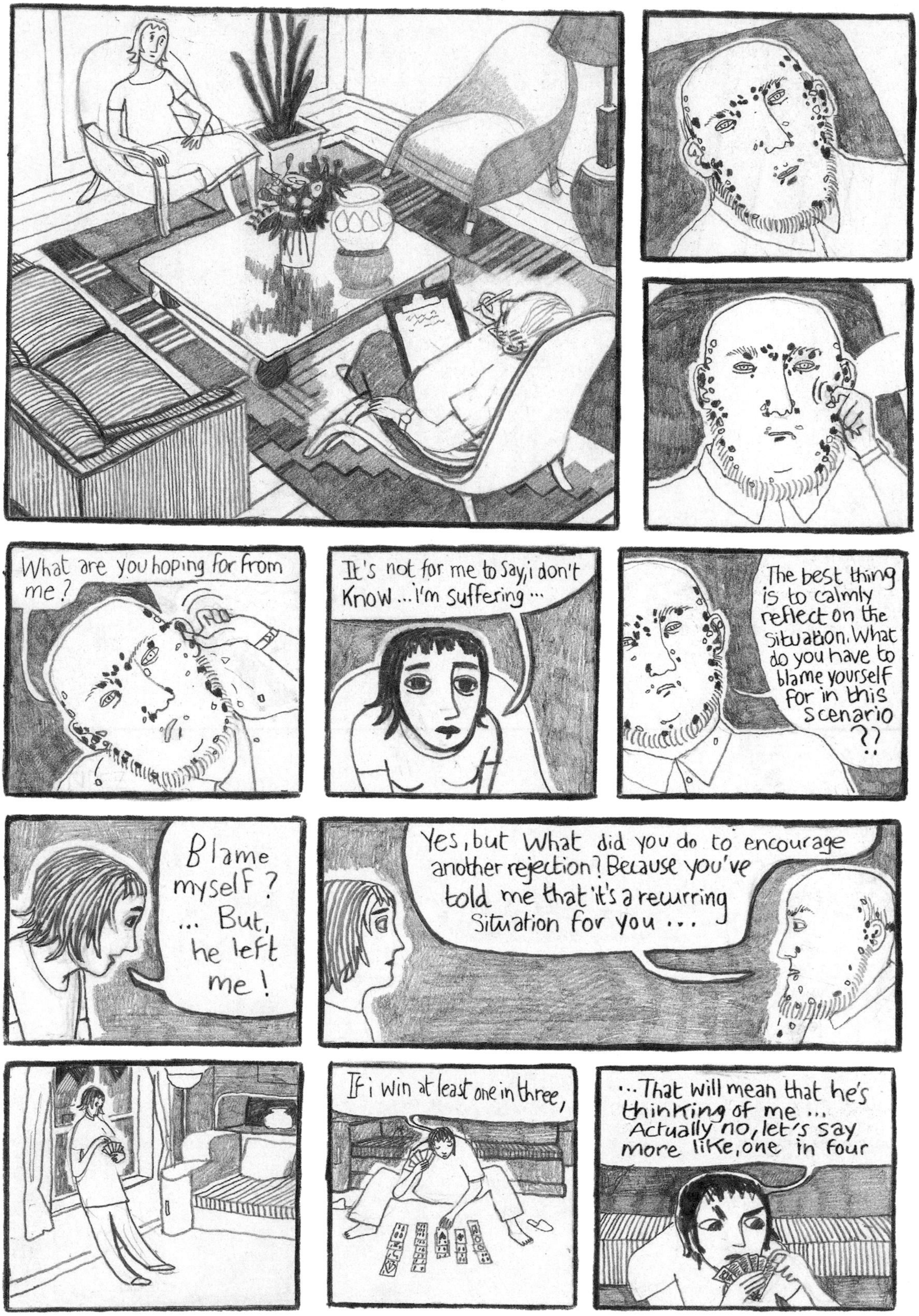
What are you hoping for from me?
It's not for me to say, i don't Know... i'm suffering...
The best thing is to calmly reflect on the situation. What do you have to blame yourself for in this scenario ??
Blame myself? ... But, he left me!
Yes, but What did you do to encourage another rejection? Because you've told me that it's a recurring situation for you...
If i win at least one in three,
...That will mean that he's thinking of me... Actually no, let's say more like, one in four

Hello!
So, how's it going today?
UFF... i found a letter this morning in my mailbox
And what's it say?
Hang on, i'll read it to you!
"I'M IN A MOMENT OF GREAT CONFUSION. I'M WORRIED BY THE PASSING OF TIME I NEED A BIT OF SOLITUDE TO RECENTER MYSELF, TO FIND MYSELF, SIMPLY TO GIVE MYSELF A LITTLE TIME. I KNOW YOU'LL UNDERSTAND."
"I KNOW YOU'LL UNDERSTAND..."
You're kidding!
And what did the therapist say?
pfff...
Okay, listen, let's go have a bite to eat together, that'll do you good!
You know... i don't have much time right now, i'm teaching in an hour, and i can't stomach a thing
But if you want, maybe we could see each other tonight?
With pleasure!
Mm... What would i do if i didn't have a friend as precious as you?!!?

We're going to continue with the negative-positive exercise
but you can work with whatever subject you like!
If you want you can flip through the magazines over on the bookcase to get ideas
I've got a little layout issue... could you come look??
yes...
i'm coming...
...in a second...

SH

How's it going?
WHAT?
How's it going?
Want something to drink?
HUH!
Want a drink?
I love this club, i'm here every weekend ... you?
Almost every day, i try to come as much as possible ...
I've almost never seen eyes like yours ... has anyone told you that you have incredible eyes?!?
Oh yeah? What i like about you is your nose!
Well, i'm exhausted
What?
I'm outta here
Do you want me to take you home?
Huh ... Okay, i came with a friend, i'll tell her i'm taking off
SYLVIA! SYLVIA!
SYLVI!
You're not going to ask me in for one last little drink?
no ... but i'll never forget you!

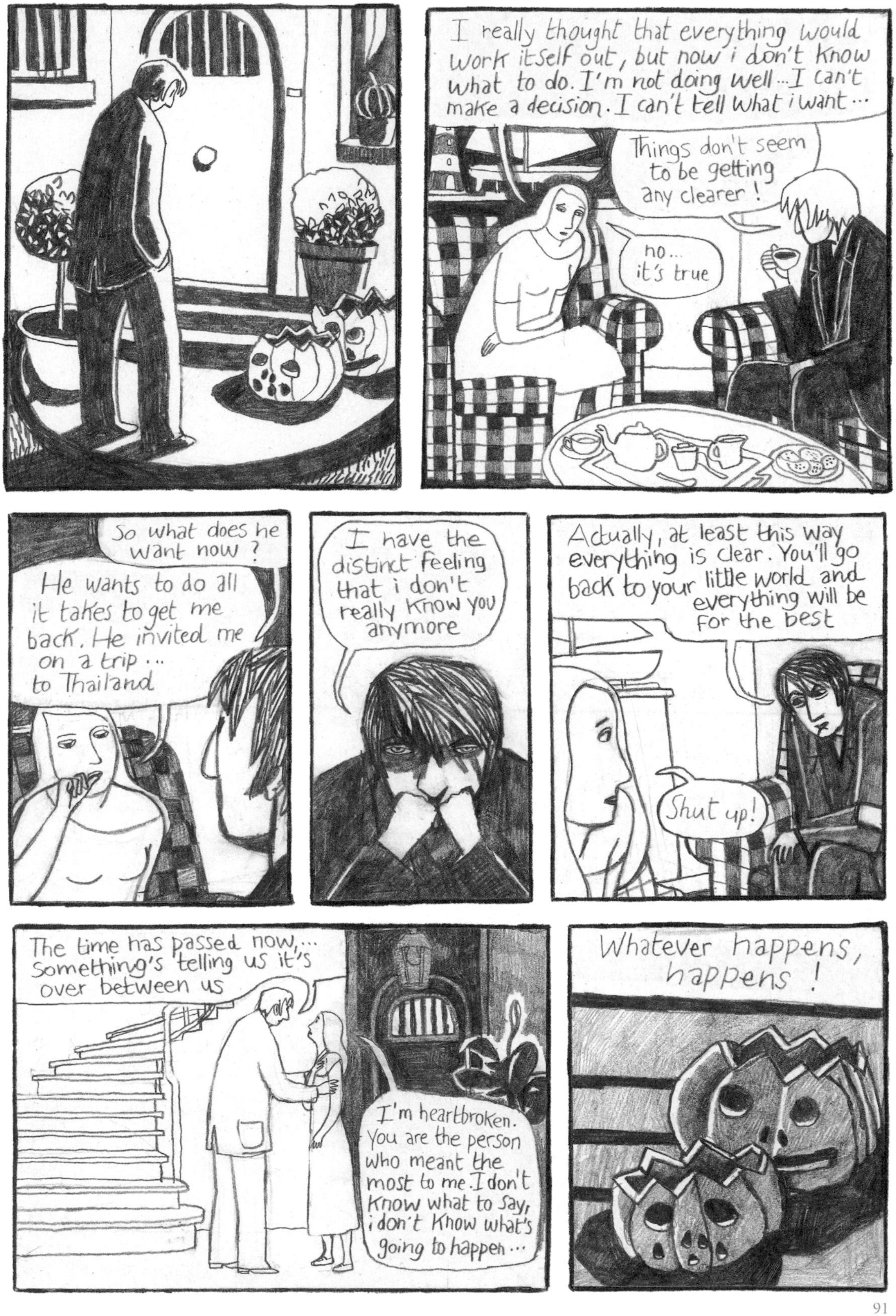

I really thought that everything would work itself out, but now i don't know what to do. I'm not doing well...I can't make a decision. I can't tell what i want...
Things don't seem to be getting any clearer !
no... it's true
So what does he want now ?
He wants to do all it takes to get me back. He invited me on a trip... to Thailand
I have the distinct feeling that i don't really know you anymore
Actually, at least this way everything is clear. You'll go back to your little world and everything will be for the best
Shut up!
The time has passed now,... something's telling us it's over between us
I'm heartbroken. You are the person who meant the most to me. I don't know what to say, i don't know what's going to happen...
Whatever happens, happens !

There's something weighing on me ...I have to talk to you about something...
What, what's happening? tell me!
... Your mother knows, ... Your grandmother knows, ... Marie knows, ...
Speak already! What's going on?
Well, um ...It's your father ...It would seem he's not doing well...
...In fact, it would seem he's really not doing well at all...
...In fact ...It would seem that he's in the hospital...
... In fact ... it would seem ... that he's dead!
What? What are you saying?? people don't seem to be dead, we're dead, or we're not dead but we can't "seem" dead...

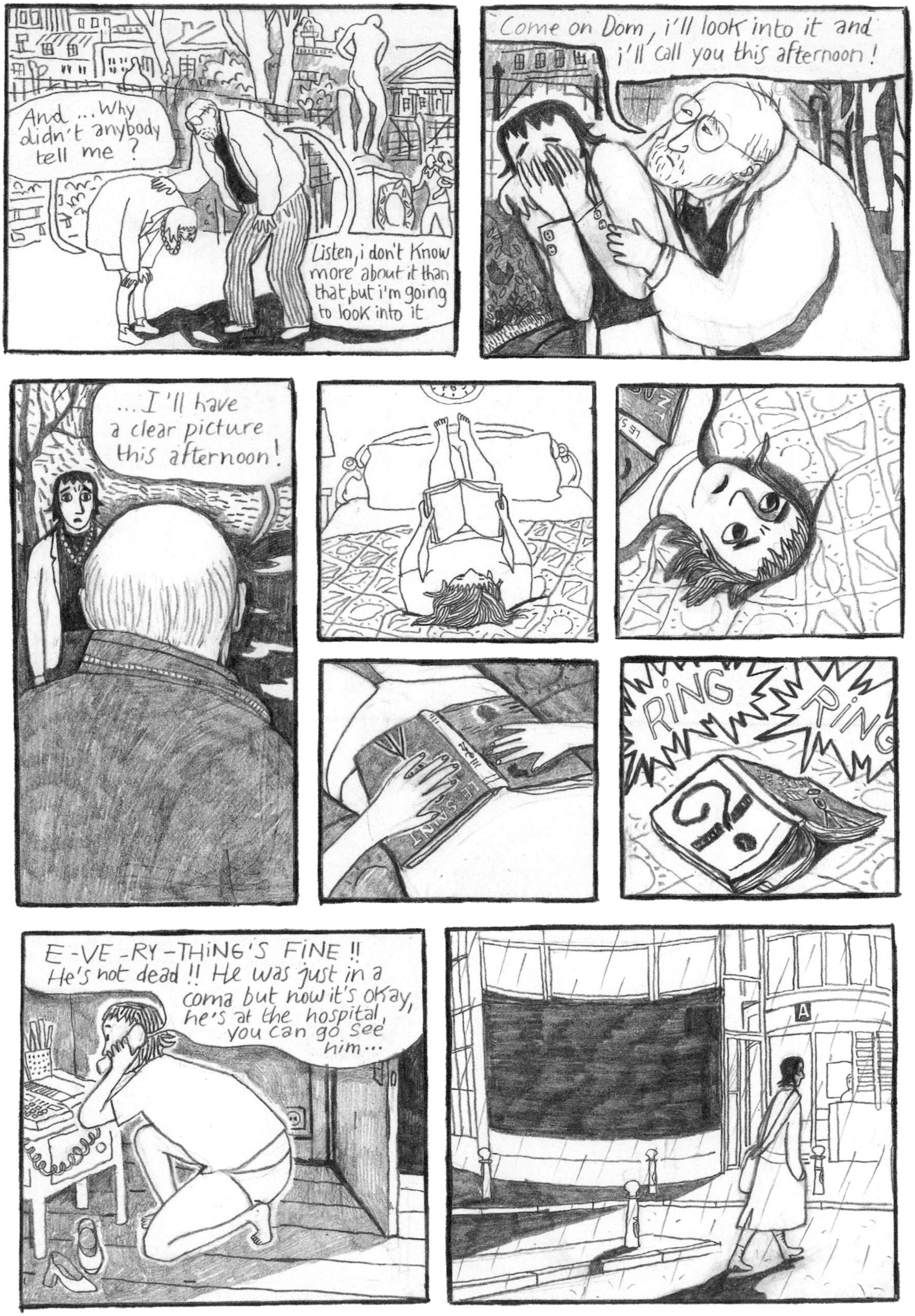

And ... Why didn't anybody tell me ?
Listen, i don't Know more about it than that, but i'm going to look into it
Come on Dom, i'll look into it and i'll call you this afternoon !
... I'll have a clear picture this afternoon !
RING
RING
E-VE-RY-THING'S FINE !! He's not dead !! He was just in a coma but now it's okay, he's at the hospital, you can go see him ...
A

I wanted a smoke...
And this is the only place we're allowed
I thought something happened to you... How horrible... How are you doing? Are you in much pain?
No, i'm fine
And there's Something else!
What's going on?

It's too much, you're unwell and i'm the one who's crying and cowardly
go on, talk!
I can't take it anymore, i loved Someone terribly ... and he left me. I don't understand why
I've been unhappy ever since ... i'm at the end ... i was with him for eight months and he left me ...
i wanted to die ...
If he left you, it's because he's not worth the trouble! Listen to what i'm going to tell you: NOBODY's worth crying over. Believe me my dear, nobody's important enough for your tears ...

JULY 8, 1998 - THE DAY OF MY BIRTHDAY
→ THE FIREFIGHTER IS DEAD

CHAPTER 3

But no Papa...
It's you who
abandoned us
VRRROOM

VROOMM
VRRRRR
RRRMMRROOM
VRMMUUUUR
VRRR
RRRROOON

RRRRRRRROOOOOM
I'm bored...
I dunno what to do...
VRROOM
VROOM
VVVVVVRRRRROOOOMM
MAKE ANOTHER DRAWING THEN
Yes, well, but you see i don't really want to!
MM
VVROOM

WHAT DO YOU WANT TO DO THEN ?
There is nothing i wanna do... i wanna go in the garden...
OUT OF THE QUESTION! CAN'T YOU SEE HOW IT'S RAINING?
VRRRR
RAOHHHH
ROOMMVROOM VRRROON
VROOMRRR
CLICK CLACK CLICK CLACK
CLICK
CLACK
CLICK
CLACK

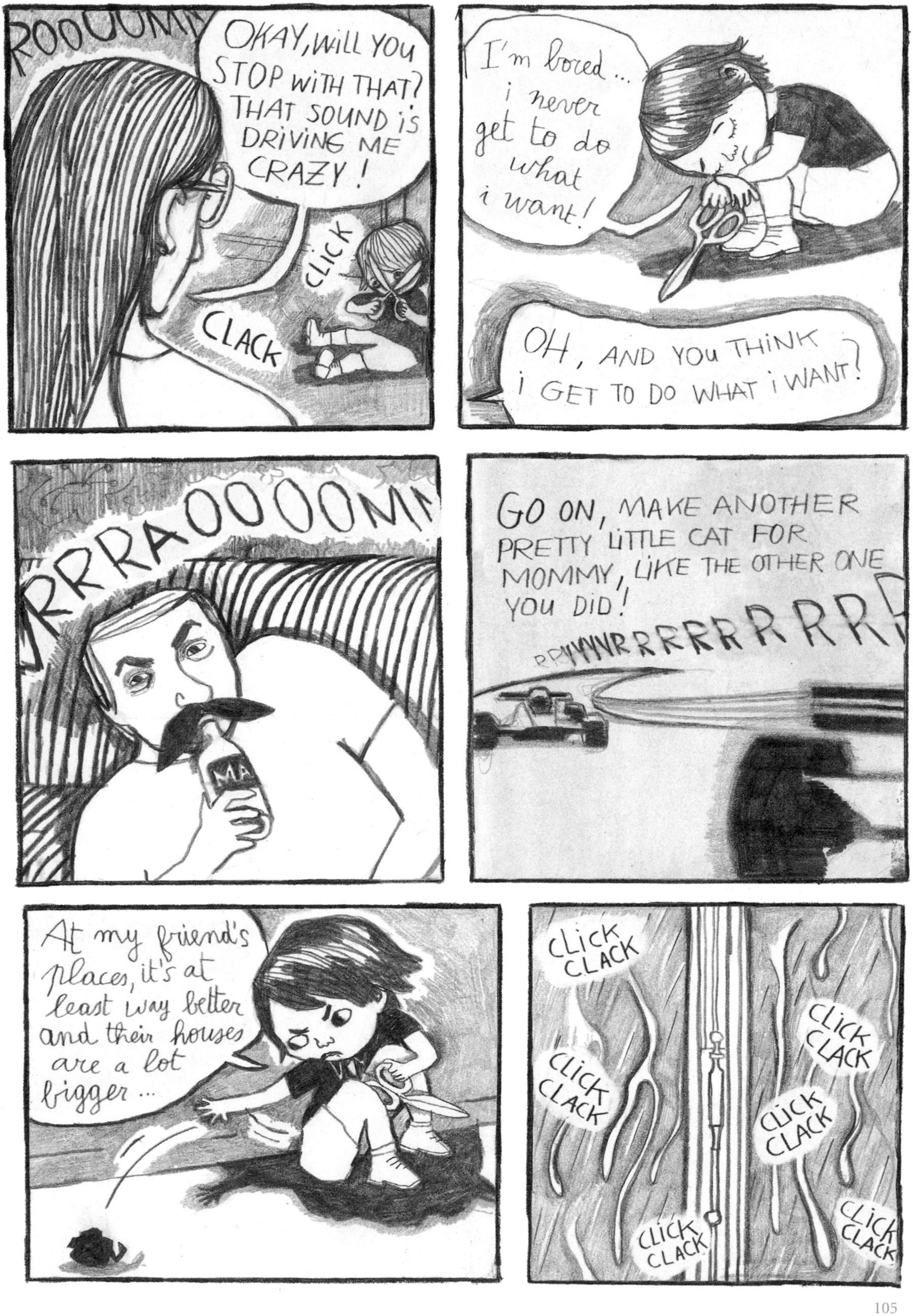
ROOOOM
OKAY, WILL YOU STOP WITH THAT? THAT SOUND IS DRIVING ME CRAZY!
CLICK
CLACK
I'm bored... i never get to do what i want!
OH, AND YOU THINK I GET TO DO WHAT I WANT?
RRRAOOOOOM
MA
GO ON, MAKE ANOTHER PRETTY LITTLE CAT FOR MOMMY, LIKE THE OTHER ONE YOU DID!
RRYYYYRRRRRRRRR
At my friend's places, it's at least way better and their houses are a lot bigger...
CLICK CLACK
CLICK CLACK
CLICK CLACK
CLICK CLACK
CLICK CLACK
CLICK CLACK

OKAY, NOW I'M FED UP!
YOU ARE GOING TO SIT AND MAKE A PAINTING... AND I WON'T HEAR ANY MORE OF IT!
EEEEEEEVVVROOOMVROOMMM
MMMVVVVVRRRRRRRRR
RRRRRRRR
TAK TAK TAK
And all my friends, they always go on vacation, and we always stay here!
I TOLD YOU TO KEEP QUIET!

VRRROOMM
MMMMVVVROOOMMM
TAK
TAK
TAK
TAK
TAK
TAK
TAK
TAK
TAK
STOP IT WITH YOUR FOOT!!
TAK
TAK

WHAT HAVE YOU DONE?
It wasn't me!
YES IT WAS YOU!
no, it wasn't me!
And there you go! this circus again!
Jesus, Mary and Joseph, When will this racket end?!
I'VE HAD ENOUGH ENOUGH ENOUGH ENOUGH
RROOOOOMMM
YOU'RE A REAL BRAT!
Hey no way...,
It's not going to go like that with me!!

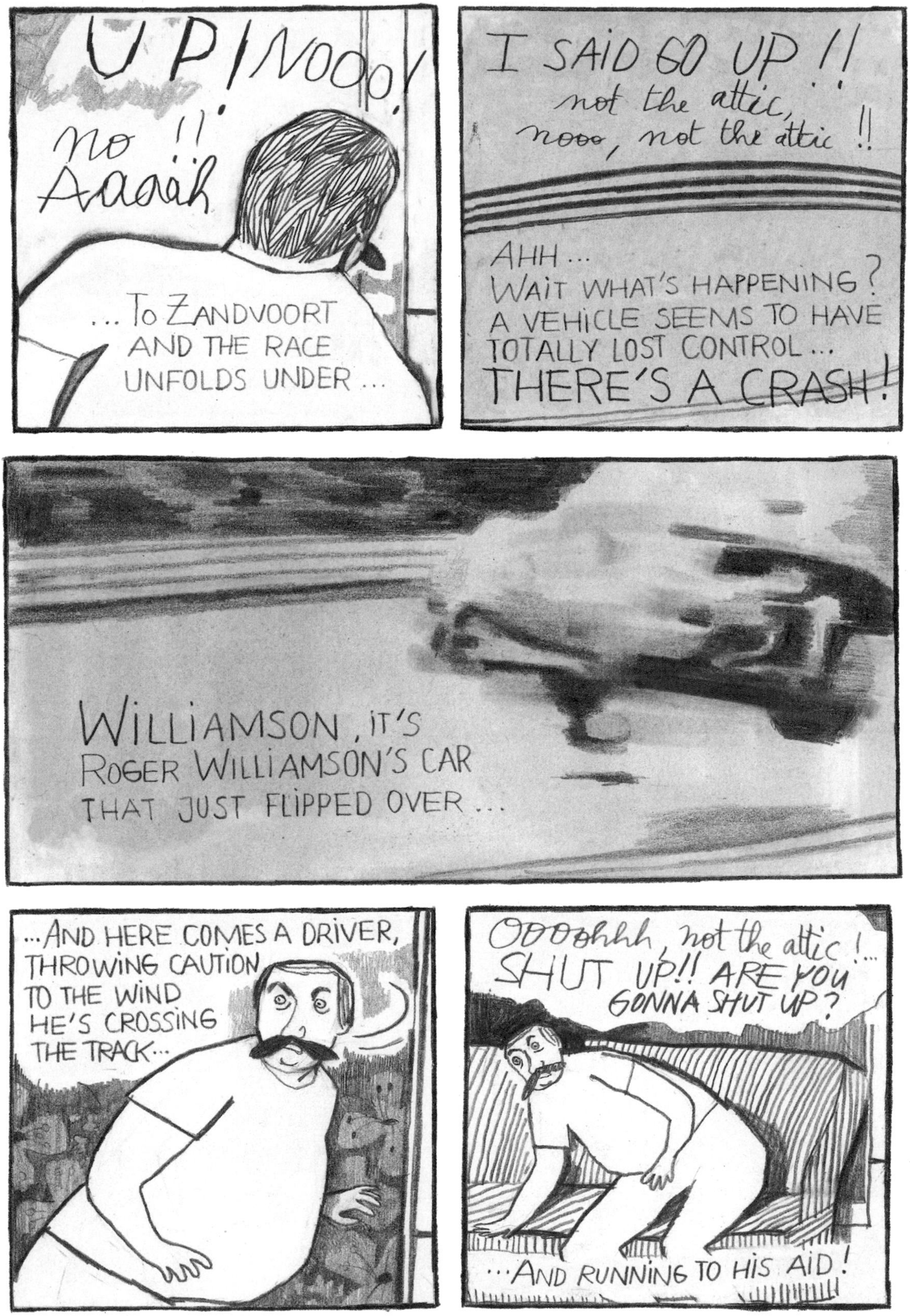
UP! NOOO!
no !! Aaaah
... To ZANDVOORT AND THE RACE UNFOLDS UNDER ...
I SAID GO UP !!
not the attic, nooo, not the attic !!
AHH ... WAIT WHAT'S HAPPENING? A VEHICLE SEEMS TO HAVE TOTALLY LOST CONTROL ... THERE'S A CRASH!
WILLIAMSON, IT'S ROGER WILLIAMSON'S CAR THAT JUST FLIPPED OVER ...
... AND HERE COMES A DRIVER, THROWING CAUTION TO THE WIND HE'S CROSSING THE TRACK ...
Ooooohhh, not the attic! ...
SHUT UP!! ARE YOU GONNA SHUT UP?
... AND RUNNING TO HIS AID!

...IT'S DAVID PURLEY!
Even here you're still capable of wreaking havoc!!
You think MAYBE I'D JUST LEAVE YOU HERE LIKE THAT?
LITTLE BRAT!

HE TRIES ALONE, IN THE FLAMES, TO TURN OVER WILLIAMSON'S CAR ... OH MY GOD, HE CAN'T REACH HIM... WHAT'S GOING ON? IT'S HORRIFYING ...
I'M GOING TO TIE YOU UP !!! THAT'S WHAT WE HAVE TO DO WITH NASTY LITTLE GIRLS LIKE YOU ...

WE HAVE TO STRING THEM UP !!!

PUT YOUR HANDS IN THE AIR!!

PUT YOUR HANDS IN THE AIR
I SAID! HIGHER!!!

TOO LATE, IT'S ALL OVER, THE FIREFIGHTERS ARRIVE ARMED WITH POWERFUL EXTINGUISHERS...
WILLIAMSON COULD NEVER HAVE SURVIVED SUCH AN INFERNO.
...LOOK HOW DAVID PURLEY SITS AT THE EDGE OF THE TRACK. HE SEEMS LOST AT SEA. THERE HE IS, HELMET IN HAND. HOPELESS...
WHAT WE'VE JUST WITNESSED, LIVE IS A TRUE TRAGEDY, A DARK DAY FOR THE WORLD OF SPORTS. FOR THE WORLD IN GENERAL.

IT'S OVER, IT'S OVER... SO LET'S STOP CRYING!
OHHOOOHOHHOOOOHHHHHHH
COME... COME HERE, UP ON MY LAP
OHHHHHHHHHHHHHHHH
IT'S OVER, IT'S OVER NOW! CALM DOWN, I'M NOT MAD ANYMORE...
OHHHHHHHHH
But... Also there was a spider and it was going to attack me!!
OHH... MY DEAR, IS THAT REALLY WHY YOU'RE CRYING?
YOU MUSTN'T BE AFRAID OF SPIDERS, LOOK... THEY SEEM A BIT FRIGHTENING BUT IN THE END YOU KNOW...
Jesus, Mary and Joseph! WHAT A WRECK! What a CATASTROPHE!

Sniff... I won't do it again! i won't ever do it again!
BUT... YES MY DEAR... i KNOW... THAT WON'T HAPPEN AGAIN ...THAT WON'T HAPPEN AGAIN...
What a circus! ... i've never seen such a thing !!
WHAT A MESS!!
Jesus, Mary'n Joseph..
WHAT A WRECK!!
But i'll tell you what huh... If i'd been there...

I would've gotten that guy out of his heap!
Not to blow my own horn but i know What needed to be done!
...CUZ ME, i'M A FIREFighTER!
But i'll tell ya... iF i'd been THERE, i'd have gotten That guy out of his heap! i GUARANTEE it one hundred percent!!
How about a little game?
Here, look we're going to play...

C'est un jeu fort répandu
* IT'S A VERY POPULAR GAME
Ne t'en fais pas!
*REGISTERED TRADEMARK
DON'T WORRY !
In any case, i didn't know about this story about the attic ... If i'd been there, Jesus and Mary, you can be sure it wouldn't have happened like that!
And ... How many times did that happen?
Um ... i don't know, a few ...
IF i'd know that! You can be sure ... Let me tell you, that i would've NEVER allowed that!
Watch it, let's not talk about this anymore, i hear Blandine and Nikita coming back!

Is her name "Bleeding"?
No NiK, She's named "Blandine"
How many croquettes?
I'll Serve MYSELF!
She's like that! She doesn't like to be served, i've never been allowed to...
Wow, how strange! i find it Charming when a man Serves me. I don't Know, maybe i'm a little bit "old France"!
OLD FRANCE! OLD FRANCE! OLD BELGIUM YEAH!
OLD FRANCE!! OLD FRANCE... I Know what is to "be" OLD FRANCE!
Yeah, that's true! She comes from a very rich family and when she was with her husband, they lived in a villa like you've never seen! They made more money than all OF US combined 5 MILLION BUCKS!!
OLD FRANCE!

Bon appetit!
mumblemumble your daughter...
What?
No, no, nothing!
Actually, yes! What did you just say? You said something about my daughter!
NO NOTHING! NOTHING AT ALL! I DIDN'T SAY ANYTHING AT ALL!
Ha well, i must have misunderstood!
Get out of here, right now!
Hey, what's the matter with you? You're not eating again??
NO i'm not eating!
Well then what are you doing? What on earth is this scene about?!?
AAAHH
IT'S HER!!

She's got no reason to be IN MY HOUSE! i WANT her to get the hell OUT OF HERE!!
Come on Nikita, We're going!
AND She ... She is staying here! She's going to stay here! She has nothing to do with all this!!
Yeah right!
DON'T TOUCH ME! YOU DON'T TOUCH ME!
Let go of my mom Bleeding!!
I'll take you home!
What's gotten into you, huh?

DOMINIQUE!!
COME BACK
DON'T DO THIS TO ME!
I really don't know what's the matter with her... Normally, she's so sweet, so kind...
Don't worry too much, it's not the end of the world!
GFS 027
She'd better not act up with me, huh?!! Or i'll throw her right out!!!
If this keeps up i'm going to become a woman-hater!
Ja wadde zeg!! What a circus!! The firefighters used to put it well: "NOTHING BETTER THAN A GOOD FRIEND!!!"

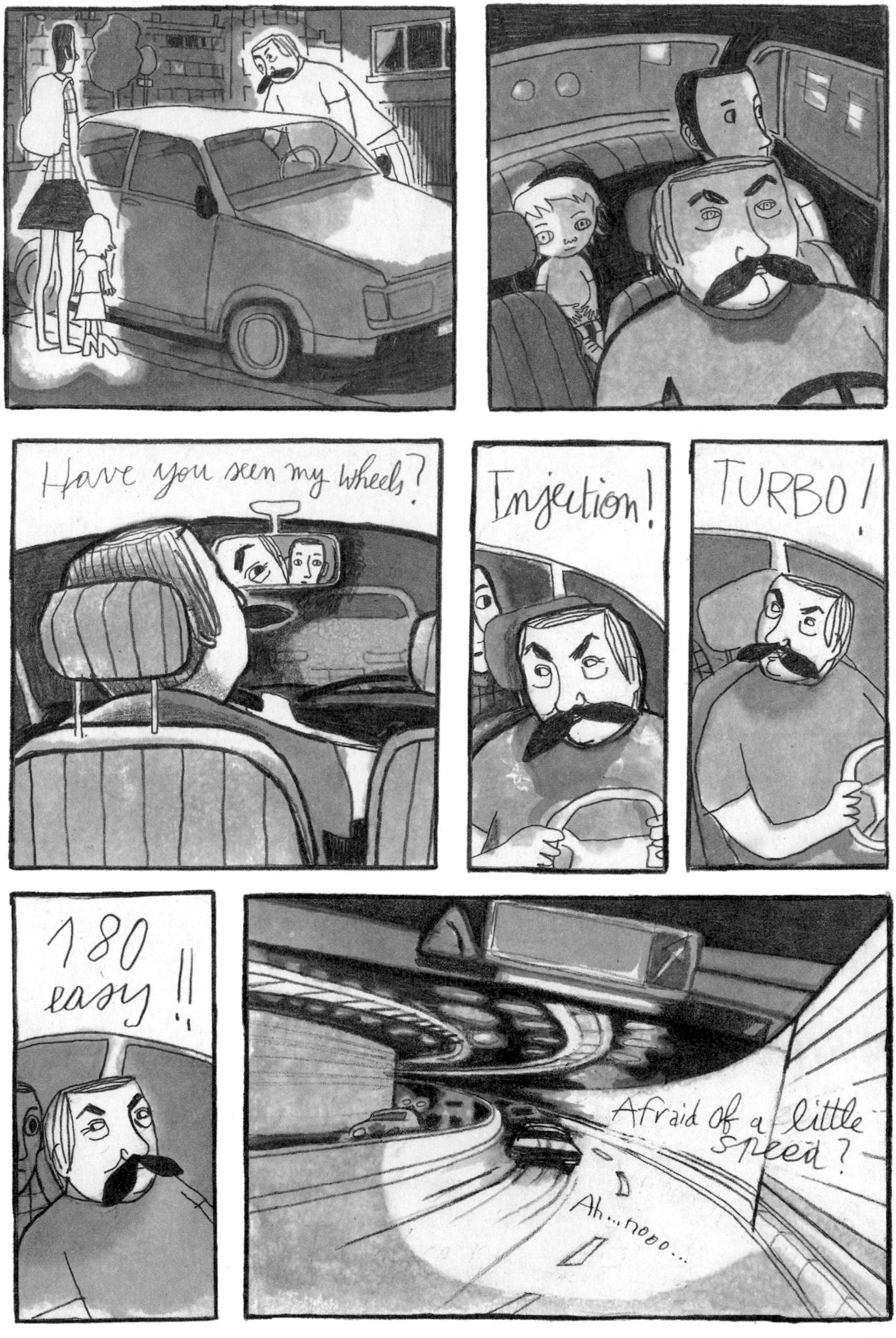
Have you seen my wheels?
Injection!
TURBO!
180 easy!!
Afraid of a little speed?
Ah...nooo...

CHAPTER 4

HHO 046
Yes?
We don't have these soles anymore, we can't fix this Kind anymore!

To me it seems totally ABSURD to have to throw out pratically new shoes on such a pretext!
new?
And why should i have to give them up if i like them?
Do you throw out the things you like?
We can't keep everything. There are times when we have to sort things out, right?
AND WHY IS THAT?
To see more clearly ... Listen, leave them with me, i'll see what i can do!
Come back a little later and i'll let you know!

NO WAY !! I've got a ton of work waiting. I can't waste my time like this !
PSR 2
VN04
PFB 5
Pfff ... This adds up to shit !
THE IMMORTAL BLIND LEMON JEFFERSON
COMIX 2000
REVOLUTION
DELEUZE
DYLAN
XENAKIS
DADA
AVANT GARDE
BRUITS
MUSIQ
I'm a cork on the ocean Floating over the raging sea...

How deep is the ocean?
I'm a rock in a landslide...
Rolling over the mountainside...
How deep is the valley?

It Kills my soul...
GRRRAOUW
Peeep
It Kills my soul...

GRRRRAAAOURRRWWWRAOUWW
THE IMMORTAL
BLIND LEMON JEFFERSON
PeeP
PeeP
QUILLET I
QUILLET I
MIII
ARRWAOUWWW
PeeeP?
I'm a leaf on a windy day...

Pretty soon I'll be blown away...
Dom?... it's me.
Hello?
Why are you calling?
I wanted to hear your voice...
Well, did you find a new apartment?
Yes, i finally moved. I'm up on the top floor now. I really like it...
Listen, i was thinking...

I...
...yes?
Something happened here. The cat brought in a bird. It's injured, i don't know what to do...
Where is it?
Where?
I have it here, in my hand, it's still breathing...
... mmm ...
I think that you could...
i'd like you to come see it...

... Listen, the cat is locked up,
i can put the bird in a box ...

And come get you, if you like?

I don't want to lie to you ... in fact ...

It just flew off...
it seemed hurt, traumatized,
almost dead,
but in the end,
it flew...

I really want to see you!

When ?

now

What does it mean to write one's own reality? This question concerning autobiography and fiction, already present in *Souvenir d'une journée parfaite** (which creates a fiction out of autobiographical elments?), turns on itself here: what part of fiction produces the singular event of focusing us on the key episodes of our own existence? We arrive here at the heart of the problem: how have we created, in ourselves, that which we consider to be our own reality? The past is fiction, re memorization, re-interpretation, fleeting obsession (based on an accepted reality), projection, hypothesis, and opacity. Our past carries memories that most often mix up what we have been told many times as if it were true (the recurring stories of our parents). How did we end up accepting this? They decide this is what will be our construction material. Secondly: what is my role, I who intervenes in a story that is supposed to be autobiography? Restructure, reinvent the relationships, so be it. But what about my character? His disturbed and deceitful appearance only escapes my own disapproval because of this stepping back that is in itself the act of writing—it's indeed a character (composed of guilt, dread, suffering, etc.) that I attempt to bring to life within the structure of the book. In this way we become intelligible and unregretful. Everything can be approached without fear or remorse. Why? Because it is not just about life itself but about Art (the omniscient, unassailable power of art). This is why GM isn't Guy Marc and the Dom of the story isn't Dominique Goblet—these are, in reality, avatars controlled by living people bearing similar names.

GUY MARC HINANT

**Memories of a Perfect Day*, Frémok, 2001.

ACKNOWLEDGMENTS

For their support all along for this book, I would like to thank a great number of people around me, my friends first: Octave, Sanam, Zab, Julie, Sjakie and Hans, Pierre Hallet, Thierry and Eve, Bernard and Sophie, Martine . . . but equally, François Schuiten, Martha the mother of Guy Marc, Barbara Stinglhamberg . . .

But above all, I would like to thank my daughter Nikita. Her invested and attentive reading, her well considered comments and especially her affection have aided me so much. Guy Marc, naturally, for his incredible openness and the complicity that we found in collaborating so closely. K54 & Kulko Limoon from the UP Krew for their intervention and creation of the graffiti and tags in "Xa's bedroom." Thierry Umbriet for his visual interpretation of an ocular migraine. Joost Pollmann for the support, the attention, the faith and the investment that he has made in my work.

Finally, my mother, for whom I have lots of love and who, I hope, will consider this book an homage.

And to finish, Jean-Christophe Menu, without whom this book wouldn't exist, and who played a role which largely surpassed that of an editor and of an exceptional friend and who, thanks to his reflections and sensible questions, pushed me, when he had to, to rethink my work, and who allowed me to go all the way with what I needed to do, truly all the way.

ALSO AVAILABLE
FROM NEW YORK REVIEW COMICS

AGONY
Mark Beyer

PEPLUM
Blutch

ALMOST COMPLETELY BAXTER
Glen Baxter

WHAT AM I DOING HERE?
Abner Dean

SOFT CITY
Pushwagner